**DO NOT REMOVE
CARDS FROM POCKET**

A Tribute to
THE YOUNG AT HEART

THE BERENSTAINS

By Julie Berg

Published by Abdo & Daughters, 4940 Viking Drive Suite 622, Edina, Minnesota 55435.

Library bound edition distributed by Rockbottom Books, Pentagon Tower, P.O. Box 36036, Minneapolis, Minnesota 55435.

Cover photo: People magazine
Photo credits: Random House pg. 5
              Wide World pgs. 10, 13
              People magazine pgs. 18, 23, 26

Edited by Rosemary Wallner

LIBRARY OF CONGRESS CATALOGING-IN-PUBLICATION DATA

Berg, Julie.
    The Berenstains / written by Julie Berg.
        p. cm. -- (Young at Heart)
    Includes bibliographical references and index.
    ISBN 1-56239-224-7
    1. Berenstain, Stan, 1923 - --Biography--Juvenile literature. 2. Berenstain, Jan, 1923- --Biography--Juvenile literature. 3. Authors, American--20th century--Biography--Juvenile literature. 4. Children's stories--Authorship--juvenile literature. I. Title. II. Series.
    PS3552.E6997Z54   1993
    813'.5409--dc20   93-12959
    [B]   CIP
                                                 AC

TABLE OF CONTENTS

A POPULAR TEAM

The husband and wife team of Stan and Jan Berenstain have created one of the most successful series of books in children's literature: The Berenstain Bears. Why are these books so successful? Some people think children read these books because they are well written. Others, however, think that clever marketing sells the books. Whatever the reason, these books are popular. Only Dr. Seuss has sold more children's books than the Berenstains.

But there is more to the Berenstain books than popularity. The stories are up-beat, colorful, and funny. And they offer hope and a positive picture of family life.

"Our world is family humor," said Stan. "I see us in the Peter Rabbit mold. Yet we don't sugar-coat life. We deal with reality."

The very popular children's book writing
team of Stan & Jan Berenstain.

JANICE & STANLEY

Janice (Jan) Grant Berenstain was born on July 26, 1923, in Philadelphia, Pennsylvania. Her father was a carpenter and a builder. But at night, he went to art school.

"My father would have his easel and drawing board set up," Jan explained, "and I was allowed to use his supplies. So I got in a lot of practice before starting school and it propelled me along."

Jan developed her art talents in school. Her teachers spotted her talent. They encouraged her.

"When we were kids, the teacher would usually adopt the one good kid in the class as 'the artist,' " she said, " and would then enlist him/her to do all the wall illustrations and things like that. So, in those days, you were sort of a professional before your time."

A love of art led Jan to the Philadelphia College of Art. Jan entered the college in 1941. There she met fellow art student Stan Berenstain.

Stanley Berenstain was born on September 29, 1923, in Philadelphia, Pennsylvania. Both he and Jan were accomplished art students by the time they met in college. They painted and did other things together. Eventually they became good friends.

Though never formally engaged, Jan and Stan planned to marry after World War II. Stan was drafted into the army where he spent nearly three-and-a-half years. Jan stayed in school and worked different jobs. She began to teach at the art school.

Toward the end of his army stint, Stan was doing medical art in a plastic surgery center in Indiana. He and Jan were about to get married. Since he had always been interested in humorous art, he decided to submit four cartoons to Norman Cousins. Cousins was the editor-in-chief of the *Saturday Review of Literature*.

Much to Stan's surprise, Cousins bought his cartoons. "The fact that he bought them came as a great shock," Stan said. "So I figured that unless I was going to continue to study painting under the GI Bill, Jan and I could make a little money here, and our collaboration evolved."

The Berenstains married on April 13, 1946. Once they broke into the family magazine market, Jan's involvement in their business partnership grew.

"I really started contributing then because we had to do domestic subjects," she explained. "And I just horned my way in."

Jan and Stan got along well. Jan drew good and funny illustrations. Slowly, the Berenstains developed a cartoon style. But for a long time, their collaboration remained a secret.

"We didn't even think there was anything unusual about our collaboration," said Stan. "It wasn't until after we sold a lot of work to the major magazines that people even knew there were two of us. Originally, I had signed the cartoons just 'Berenstain.'

Then, when an editor in New York met us in person, he said, 'You mean there are two of you?' We said, 'Sure,' and he suggested that we change our signature to 'The Berenstains,' because it would be terrific marketing."

The Berenstains did just that. The two artists attracted much attention. As a result, the Berenstains began doing magazine covers.

"We were probably the youngest cover artists at the time working for a national magazine," said Stan. "We specialized in panoramic scenes of family adventures like going to the zoo, company picnics, and dancing school."

THE BERENSTAINS MEET DR. SEUSS

The Berenstains felt they could not rely on magazine work to support themselves. So they decided to focus their attention on another area: children's books.

Dr. Seuss books are among the favorite books
of Stan & Jan Berenstain and their children.

"At this time," Stan said, "we were busy cartoonists doing humorous art for all the big magazines. We also had kids who liked to read a lot. Whenever we would go to New York to visit the magazines, I would ask my older son what I could bring back for him to read. He wanted a funny book.

"So we began buying Dr. Seuss books because they were among the few funny books being done for kids," he continued. "Once we perceived that there weren't many robust, laugh-out-loud books for kids, we thought, 'There's a niche that might be fun to enter.' "

Also at that time, the Berenstains had a running magazine cartoon called, "It's All in the Family." Since they were doing family humor for grown-ups, they thought they could do it for children.

THE BERENSTAIN BEARS

The first Berenstain books were published in a series called "Beginner Books." Theodor Seuss Geisel (Dr. Seuss) had started the series with *The Cat in the Hat.* The Berenstain books encouraged children to read.

They were written in rhyme, and were very funny. Dr. Seuss was the editor.

The first Berenstain Bear book was *The Big Honey Hunt* (1962). It is the story of a well-meaning Papa bear who tries to impress his wide-eyed son with his wisdom. But his efforts only end in comical disasters.

The original bears were rough-looking but gentle creatures. Mama bear wore a polka-dot bonnet. Papa dressed in bib overalls. And they lived in a tree house with their bouncy little cub. (Sister Bear didn't become part of the bear family until 1974). More than two decades later, the Bears still wear some of the same clothing.

"We hoped we'd have a series from it," Stan said, "but it wasn't up to us. Our editor said, 'Why don't you try something different?' "

The Berenstains wrote another book called *Nothing Ever Happens at the South Pole*. The book was about a penguin who has a diary tossed into his igloo by a mailman. A message on the front of the diary said to write something in it everyday.

The original Berenstain Bears were rough-looking
creatures but always gentle and funny .

So the penguin walks around the South Pole looking for things to write about. All these terrible things happen behind his back, but the penguin doesn't see them. At the end of the diary, he writes, "Nothing ever happens at the South Pole."

The Berenstains did the sketches for the book and brought them to their publisher. But then Theodor Geisel told them that their first Berenstain Bear book was doing really well. He suggested that they write another.

The Berenstains did just that. Soon the "Bear Books," as they were called, dominated their professional lives. "After that, it was just bears, bears, bears," said Stan. "Incidentally, that penguin book has never been published."

The Berenstains chose to illustrate bears because they are the ideal characters for children's books. "The most popular creatures in children's books are bunnies and bears," said Jan. "Bunnies because they're cuddly and cute and bears because they tend to do things standing up.

"Part of the reason we chose bears is that they look good in clothes!" she added. "You can dress them up and they're fun to draw."

Coming up with the name "The Berenstain Bears" was another story. For their second Bear book, *The Bike Lesson,* Geisel decided to put a line on the cover. It read: "Another Adventure of the Berenstain Bears." The name stuck. "We never really would have thought of it," said Jan.

The Berenstains believe they would not have achieved their level of success without the help of Dr. Seuss.

"It was hard in the beginning to know what kind of impact our books were having at the other end of the sales force," said Stan. "All we ever heard was that they were doing very well. *The Cat in the Hat* had generated an enormous amount of momentum for the 'Beginner's' series. So we had the advantage of being part of a very successful line of books.

"There just weren't many books around like the ones by (Geisel) or us," he added. "Our books were broadly funny, not just cute and sweet, but wildly slapstick. And the kids liked them."

Dr. Seuss also had a strong influence over the Berenstains' simple style. He wanted simple illustrations with nothing in the background. The purpose of the books was to help children tie the pictures in with the words.

"He had a wild and wacky approach that we liked and went along with," Stan said. "The pages of the books had to be very simple. They used something called 'Beginner Book type' which was two to three times the size of the type used in our current books."

Because the words took up so much room, it was hard to design characters to fit the limited space. So the Berenstains drew tall, thin bears. Illustrating these books was completely different than working for the magazines, however.

"Except for the full paintings we did for the *Colliers* covers," said Stan, "all our magazine work had been in black and white.

We had to ask specifically for a color if we needed one. Furthermore, we were working in a tiny space. A gag cartoon is no more than two-and-three-quarter by three-and-three quarter inches. Though we didn't work that small, we always had to keep that reduction in mind. The return to conventional space and full color in our books really meant coming back to our original training."

THE BEARS' MANY FACES

The Berenstains take pride in their approach to drawing. "If you look through one of our books," Stan said, "there are probably hundreds of bear faces. I doubt two of them would be the same, which is not the usual technique for children's books. Normally those animals are expressionless or smiling, and are portrayed realistically. A rabbit looks like a rabbit."

The Berenstains create their bears completely out of their own vision and methods. They don't look like real bears. Nor do they look like teddy bears. But letters from children say that they can always tell how the Berenstain Bears feel or what they are going through.

Stan & Jan as the Berenstain Bears.

"It's been a long, twenty-five-year process of finding what works for the kinds of stories we want to do," said Stan.

THE FIRST TIME BOOKS

In 1974, the Berenstains published *The Berenstain Bears' New Baby.* They followed that book in 1978 with *The Berenstain Bears Go to School.* With these books, the Berenstains established another series for their beloved bears. It was called "The First Time Books."

"We reached another level of popularity once we started the 'First Time Books', the series we do almost exclusively now," said Stan. "These books are about first-time experiences and are a total departure from our earlier line of books."

The books are not meant to teach kids how to read. Instead, they are meant to be read and enjoyed. They include situations many children have been in. "They aren't slapstick," Stan said. "They are an attempt by us to portray a nuclear family: a father, mother, and a couple of kids."

'The First Time Books' tell what to expect from an experience. The books describe what may happen at a certain time of life, such as on the first day of school. By showing children what to expect, the books help kids feel better prepared for the event before it happens. "I think there should be more books like that for grown-ups," Stan said.

When they started the line in 1981, the books were going to be about experiences such as going to the doctor and the dentist, moving, and having a baby sitter. The Berenstains figured they would do about eight or ten books and then run out of ideas.

But that didn't happen. The books evolved into more general experiences such as Thanksgiving or getting a pet. The books also have changed their appearance. The Berenstains' early works were hardcover books. The First Time Books are in paperback.

Attention to detail is also important to the Berenstains. "We never try to skimp on detail in our pictures," said Stan. "The readers enjoy getting as much information as they can from illustrations.

Creating a real place with clarity and a good balance between words and pictures is equally important. We work very hard to make our pictures 'read.' "

Apparently, the pictures do just that. When children write letters to the Berenstains, they often comment about the pictures. "They're more alert to the content of pictures than adults," said Stan. "The first reading they do is of pictures. They don't get to language and words for a long time."

WHERE DO THEY GET THEIR IDEAS?

When it comes to subject matter, the Berenstains are choosy. They stay away from religious issues. And though they get many requests to write books on divorce, drugs, and death, they stay away from those topics as well. "We have a lot of humor in our books," Jan explained. "And there's nothing funny about those situations."

Much of the Berenstains' subject matter comes directly from their personal experiences. A 1964 book about riding a bike (*The Bike Lesson*) came from teaching their sons to ride.

In the story, Dad Bear gives Small Bear a new bike. But before he does, Dad Bear decides to ride it himself to show Small Bear how it is done. But Dad Bear wheels into a series of disasters, and Small Bear must ride Dad Bear home on the handlebars.

The Berenstain Bears and the Messy Room (1983) also came from their experiences as parents.

In the story, the room that Brother and Sister Bear share remains a mess because they argue who should clean it up instead of working together. Mama Bear loses her temper and tosses all her children's possessions into a carton that she intends to throw on the junk pile.

In real life, the Berenstains' two boys collected everything from cicada shells to birds' nests. And their rooms were disaster areas.

Stan & Jan Berenstain with their son, Michael. Many of the Berenstains' ideas come directly from their personal experiences.

Finally, Jan had to take charge. "She was Papa Bear in reality and rearranged their closet," Stan said.

Talking to young parents has also helped the Berenstains to think of things to write about. "When we were young," said Jan, "supermarkets didn't have piles of candy at the checkout counter. But we've learned since that this has become a really big problem. So *The Berenstain Bears Get the Gimmies* had to do with that. . .kids throwing tantrums at the checkout counter."

The Berenstains also began thinking about writing books for older readers. They received requests from children who wanted to keep reading about the Bears even when they got older. But the Berenstains felt that a picture book for older children was not a good idea.

Instead, they thought of doing a paperback line with black-and-white illustrations, and with more words and pages. "We might very well deal with more serious subjects in those books," Jan said.

HOW DO THEY WRITE
SO MANY BOOKS?

Because the Berenstains produce so many books, they have developed a system that allows them to work effectively together. When a book idea is presented, they both have to like it, or the project is shelved.

"That was very important early on, especially in the cartoon business," said Stan. "I might do a gag I thought was funny, but would turn out to be alone in that opinion. Sometimes I'll come up with a dumb idea and Jan will say, in a nice way, 'Gee, let's put that aside.' The next day I'll realize how dumb it was."

Both Stan and Jan think up story ideas. Whoever thinks of a story first writes down all the text. Then Stan organizes the words and pictures on layout paper. Jan usually does the pencil drawings and Stan applies the ink.

If there's more than one project, Jan will apply the ink and they will both color the illustrations.

Stan & Jan Berenstain, hard at work in their home workshop. This is where they think up their stories and create their illustrations.

By then, the editor has approved the manuscript. The Berenstains complete any final editing by talking with the editor on the phone.

THE TV BEARS

Besides their books, the Berenstain Bears have made other appearances. Since 1979, five NBC specials (which also have appeared on HBO for the last several years) have been made. The Bears also appeared on 26 half-hour shows for CBS Saturday mornings. Those cartoons are shown around the world, and are also available on videocassette.

"There are people who want us to do more television," Stan said. "And we might, though we're really very content with doing books. If a book is bad, we can't blame anybody but ourselves."

The Berenstains tend to stay away from television. The process of getting on television is different from getting published. There are hundreds of book publishers to send material to.

The Berenstains have spent much time preparing sample drawings to send to publishers. They know that sooner or later a publishing house will accept their idea. With television, however, there are only three major networks (NBC, CBS, ABC). If they don't like the project, you don't get on television.

But even if you do get on television, there are other pitfalls. "In television, the terms of success are ratings," Stan said. "There are no other considerations. Either you win your time slot or you lose it.

"Getting started is very difficult," he added. "You start with a 'selling bible' for the network, which explains the series concept, how it works, and that a lot of stories will be coming out of the characters."

Then a "writer's bible" is prepared. This is used to familiarize television writers with the characters so they can write the scripts. "It's exhausting," Stan said.

It took nine months and 15,000 drawings to produce the first show, "The Berenstain Bears' Christmas Tree." It aired on NBC on December 3, 1979. The show won its time slot by a large margin. The *New York Times* reviewed it favorably.

"We now have an interesting idea for a theatrical movie to which our agent is trying to attract producers," Stan said. "There's some interest. But that's such a large, complicated business that you never know what's going to happen. We're also doing a lot of merchandising with games, clothing, and toys based on our characters. We just want to make sure that it's done carefully. That's why we design everything ourselves."

LOOKING TO THE FUTURE

Meanwhile, the Berenstains concentrate on producing more books. Though they have many to their credit, they are not worried about running out of ideas.

"Back in the cartoon days," said Stan, "we had to come up with twenty, twenty-five cartoons a week—week in and week out. So we were depending upon ideas coming. And if we didn't, we were out of business. That training helped. Besides, what we are doing isn't [different]. Our family is a very normal one. And our bear family is very much like us. As life goes on, it keeps proposing new ideas."

One thing is certain: Kids like the Berenstain Bear books. As long as the Berenstains keep writing, children will keep reading and enjoying them.

GLOSSARY

Cartoonist — Someone who draws cartoons.

Collaboration — Two or more people working together.

Editor — A person who reads through written material. An editor corrects the material so it is ready to be printed.

Feature — A prominent article in a newspaper or magazine.

Manuscript — A book written by hand or typed. An author sends a manuscript to the publisher who makes it into a printed book.

Panoramic — A picture or series of pictures representing a continuous scene.

Paperback — A book having a flexible paper binding.

Slapstick — Comedy featuring collisions, falls, and other horseplay.

INDEX